A Zebra Plays Zither

An Animal Alphabet and Musical Revue

Written and Illustrated by Janice Bond

Pomegranate **kids**

PORTLAND, OREGON

An aged **Alligator**
artistically squeezes
Accordion solos
in time with sea breezes

Ballads befitting
two boisterous Bears
are blown forth on Bagpipes
in bellows and blares

Crickets create
a concerto divine
on Clarinet and Cornets
in blue columbine

Dazzling **Dragonflies**
Drum playfully,
delivering ditties
with dizzying glee

An **Elephant** honks
a **Euphonium** tune
encircled by eggplants
one bright afternoon

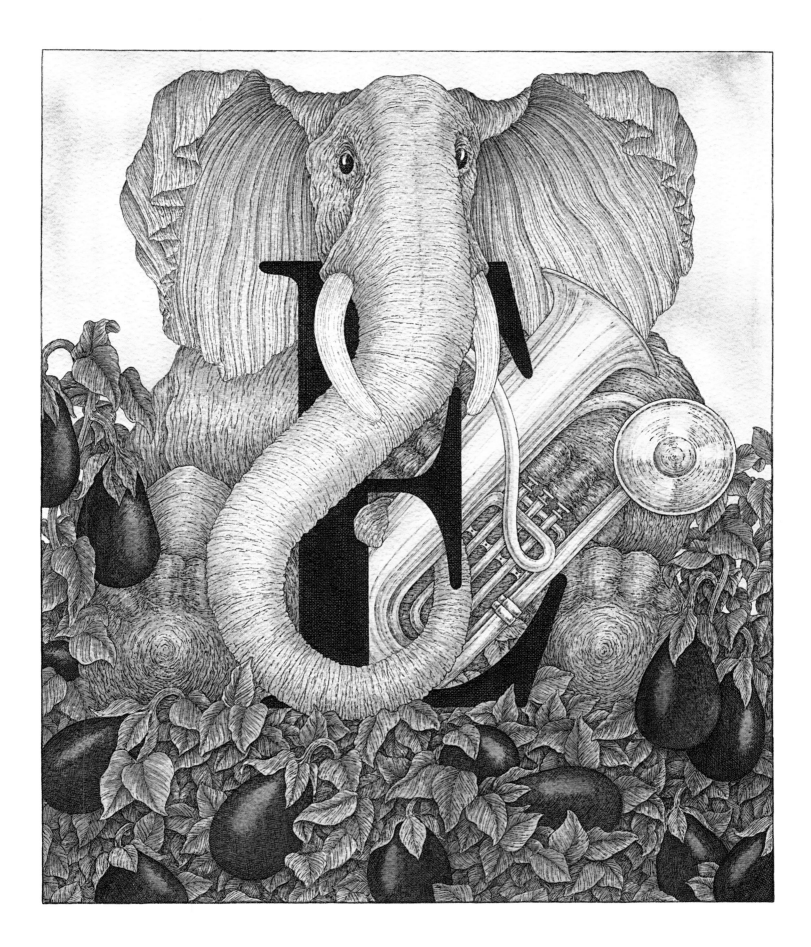

Four fancy **Fishes**
with fluorescent skins
play fun **Flute** fantasias
with fabulous fins

A gentle Giraffe
with a garland of flowers
plucks a Guitar
to while away hours

A handsome blue Heron
handily brings
harmonic inventions
to slender Harp strings

Insects on ivy
illuminate night
with sweet invocations
on Instruments bright

Gelatinous Jellyfish
jingle and jangle
with Jumbles of bells
they jauntily dangle

In a meadow of flowers
a mom Kangaroo
blows a duet
with her kid on Kazoo

A Lizard plays Lyre
alongside a Llama
whose lyrical Lute
creates musical drama

Melodious Mice
strum lullabies sweet
on small Mandolins
with the claws on their feet

Nightingales nestle
with notions of singing
silvery notes
in the **Nocturne** they're winging

Owls in oak trees
ornately convey
orchestral odes
on Oboes all day

Puffins and **Parrots**
parade by the pair
and play Percussion
with loud, rhythmic flair

Quirky Quirquinchos*
can cleverly fashion
quickstep concertos
with Quinteted passion

*pronounced keer-KEEN-chos

A **Rhinoceros** revels
in glad repartee
on **Recorder** with redbirds
who happen her way

While sunflowers sway
back and forth with the tone
a splendiferous **Snake**
blows a sleek **Saxophone**

A trio of Turtles
in rhythmic debut
toot Tuba and Trumpet
and Trombone for you

The Ukulele,
this Unicorn's choice,
adds uncommon backup
to his unique voice

A virtuoso Vixen
in violets vast
bows Violin solos
with skill unsurpassed

A wonderful Walrus
with whisker and tusk
taps whimsies on Washboard
from dawn until dusk

X-rays exchange
an exuberant tone
as they swim up and down
a long Xylophone

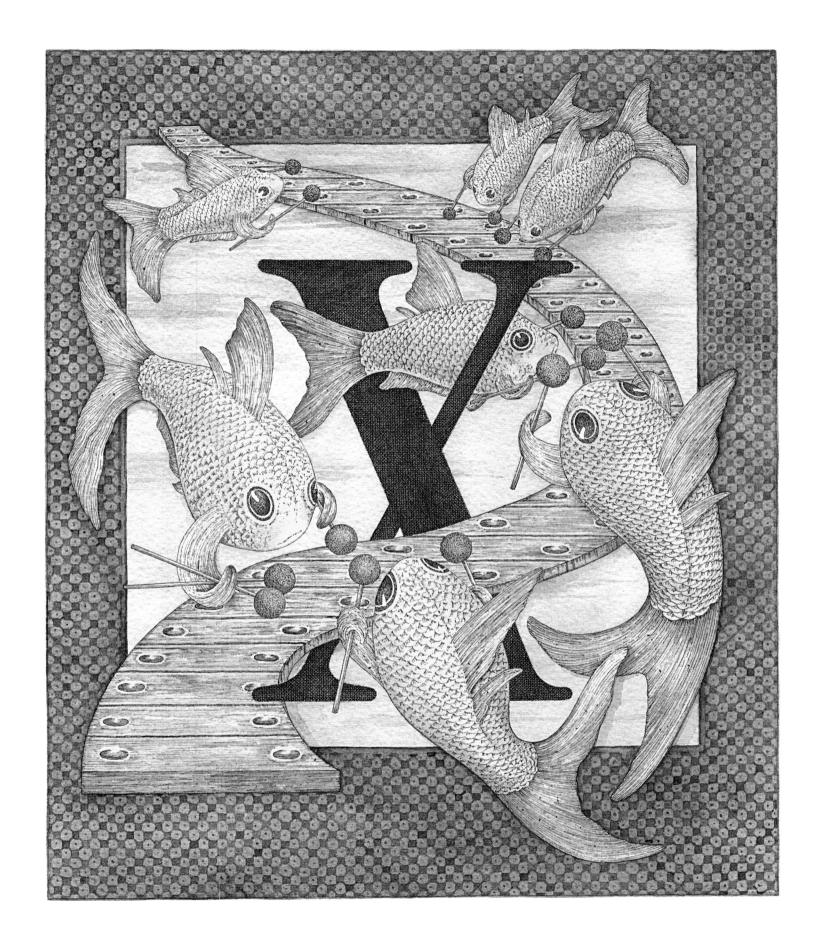

Young Yellow warblers
(birds of a feather)
have a great yen
to Yodel together

A zig-zaggy Zebra
gets many a thrill
playing his Zither
on zinnia hill

About Janice Bond

Written and illustrated by Janice Bond, this animal alphabet and musical revue was inspired by her love of illuminated letters and language, pen and ink, and watercolor. Bond is also a printmaker. She studied art at Luther College in Decorah, Iowa, and at Western Washington University in Bellingham, Washington. Bond lives, works, and creates in Portland, Oregon. She used pen and ink with watercolor to draw and paint the animals and instruments in this book.

Published by PomegranateKids®, an imprint of
Pomegranate Communications, Inc.
19018 NE Portal Way, Portland, OR 97230
800-227-1428   www.pomegranate.com

Pomegranate Europe
Number 3 Siskin Drive
Middlemarch Business Park
Coventry, CV3 4FJ, UK
+44 (0)24 7621 4461   sales@pomegranate.com

To learn about new releases and special offers from Pomegranate, please visit
www.pomegranate.com and sign up for our email newsletter. For all other queries,
see "Contact Us" on our home page.

This product is in compliance with the Consumer Product Safety Improvement Act
of 2008 (CPSIA) and any subsequent amendments thereto. A General Conformity
Certificate concerning Pomegranate's compliance with the CPSIA is available on
our website at www.pomegranate.com, or by request at 800-227-1428. For additional
CPSIA-required tracking details, contact Pomegranate at 800-227-1428.

Library of Congress Control Number: 2019930561

ISBN 978-0-7649-8651-2

Pomegranate Item No. A284
Designed by Sophie Aschwanden
Printed in China

28 27 26 25 24 23 22 21 20 19   10 9 8 7 6 5 4 3 2 1